DEDICATION

I want to thank my husband Steven Tickle for his support and patience during the writing of this book. I love you and you are appreciated. I want to thank Author's Oakley Dean and Doris Baldwin from The Baldwin Stories for all their help and support. I want to thank my lifelong friend Karen Reed for her support and being my sounding board as needed during the writing of this book. I love you and you will always be in my prayers.

Furthermore, I want to thank all the agents who supported my career, Megan Wilson, Bill Weisband and Kim Mack to name a few. I love you guys and you will always be in my thoughts and prayers. Finally, I want to thank my family. I wouldn't be who I am today without you all.

INTRODUCTION

I am Carol Tickle formerly AKA Cat, the owner and agent of Bad Girlz Bail Bonds LLC in Manassas, Virginia. As a single mother too four children, I started a bail bond business, Bad Girlz Bail Bonds LLC, in which I owned and operated from April of 2011 until I sold the business January of 2020 after becoming the wife of the outlaw Moonshiner Tickle.

The following biography is about the path that led to my career as one of the best female Bounty Hunters on the east coast. This book is the first of a series, in which I share my struggles becoming a respected Bounty Hunter in a male dominated career. I share true, tragic, scary, and sometimes thrilling events that happened during the first few years of my career as the owner and agent of Bad Girlz Bail Bonds LLC. All fugitives, agents and loved one's names have been omitted for privacy. All fugitives are considered innocent until proven guilty in a court of law.

TABLE OF CONTENTS

Table of Contents

CHAPTER 1

THE LANDLORD 5

CHAPTER 2

THE BROKEN PATH TO BAIL 9

CHAPTER 3

CHANGES 14

CHAPTER 4

BECOMING AN AGENT 18

CHAPTER 5

FRESH START 23

CHAPTER 6

FIRST RESPONDERS 30

CHAPTER 7

NO TWO DAYS THE SAME 33

CHAPTER 8

MY FIRST REVOCATION 38

CHAPTER 9

THE INCEST CASE 46

CHAPTER 10

DOUBLE CROSS 58

CHAPTER 11	
BUS DRIVER	65
CHAPTER 12	
MEGAN	70
CHAPTER 13	
ROOKIE MISTAKE	74
CHAPTER 14	
FANTASY	82
CHAPTER 15	
PIZZA BOY	91
CHAPTER 16	
THE METH LAB	95
CHAPTER 17	
RUNAWAY	107
CHAPTER 18	
MY CHRISTMAS GIFT	112
CHAPTER 19	
THE SPLIT AND RECONCILIATION	117
CHAPTER 20	
HANDICAPPED AND ELDERLY	120
CHAPTER 21	
GETTING NOTICED	125
SOURCES & CONTACT INFORMATION	129

CHAPTER 1

THE LANDLORD

It was the month of October in the year of 2010, I was a single mother to four children, three boys and one girl ranging in age from eighteen to twelve years old. I became a mother at the age of sixteen and had three children by the age of nineteen and gave birth to my fourth child at the age of twenty-one. My eldest son was joining the U.S. Air Force, my second son was battling drug addiction, my third son was quiet and stayed to himself and my daughter was struggling socially and academically in school.

We were living in an old run down home, with affordable rent and I was dealing with a shady landlord. The type that stops by unannounced and looks through your window to tell you that you need to do laundry. He knew I was a licensed real estate agent when I rented the home. He was aware I knew all about landlord tenant laws and he pushed every button he could to see if I would say something about his behavior.

I put up with these type of landlords for several years because even though I had made a great living in real estate, my credit suffered due to a divorce, poor money management and I was going through an unexpected audit with the Internal Revenue Service (IRS). The landlord filed for eviction due to nonpayment around October 2010 and a sheriff showed up at my door ready to throw me out. This took me by complete surprise because I hadn't received any notice of a court hearing and my rent was indeed paid.

I knew I should have received notice of a court hearing and was feeling like my landlord removed the notice from my door before I could see it. He did have a habit of stopping by my house all the time when I wasn't home, as mentioned before. He would always send me texts letting me know one way or another that he had been there.

There I am, barefoot on my porch, the leaves are falling off the trees, there is a slight breeze, and the air is cold. I can smell the neighbor's fireplace burning and hear a bus pull up and come to a stop. I can hear the neighborhood kids running with excitement home from school, and as they pass my driveway they settle down and try not to look. My kids walk up and there is a county car in my driveway with a sheriff demanding I leave the home, perfect timing! I was concerned my children's friends would see the sheriff and my kids would deal with harassment the next day at school.

I explained to the sheriff there must have been a mistake because I paid my rent, and I showed him the cashed check. I had just received my bank statement that day in the mail. I wasn't one to check my mail daily unless I was expecting a check. No good news ever came in the mail. He advised me to go to the clerk's office and file for an emergency hearing and that I needed to do it right now. If I had not had that proof, he would have thrown us out on the street right then and there. He was intimidating with his large build, badge, gun and hand cuffs and his attitude said he had heard it all before and had zero tolerance. I got into my car and went straight to the clerk's office. I arrived five minutes before they closed and explained what was going on.

The clerk gave me the paperwork to fill out and took a copy of the cashed rent check to add to my complaint and gave me a court date. I was shaking, mad, upset and stressed at the thought my children and I may have to leave our home, it was undeserving with no notice. I had decided at that point I will no longer stay in my lease with this landlord. The case was scheduled for an emergency hearing that got me in front of the judge the following week. The Judge vacated the order and continued the case until December. We were no longer in danger of being thrown out of our home. However, I was determined to move when the case was finalized and I would ask the judge to allow me to terminate the remainder of my lease, without financial penalty, due to the false judgement filed.

I had filed my own Bankruptcy papers in the past, and the Bankruptcy Judge was highly impressed with my work. When you're truly bankrupt you can't afford someone else to do some typing for you. This landlord messed with the wrong single mother. I may have appeared weak but weak was not who I am. I wasn't some woman he could push around, and he was about to find out how strong and smart I am. I knew I had been wronged and I was looking forward to my day in court.

CHAPTER 2

THE BROKEN PATH TO BAIL

Nearing the end of 2010 and the end of my booming real estate career, I became a victim of domestic assault. I was out with my boyfriend at a bar. We had decided to leave early, it was still daylight and we had only been there maybe an hour. We got into a disagreement in the car, I cannot remember what it was about. I do remember he was angry and driving crazy and I wanted out. When he pulled up to a stop sign, I took the opportunity to jump out of the car. I started running down the street, the opposite direction he was headed, wearing high heels and a skirt.

I tried to hide behind a vehicle while he was trying to turn his vehicle around. I was hunched down between two cars waiting to see his car pass by. My heart was beating fast, I knew it wasn't safe to be with this man. His display of anger in the car was the reason I jumped out. I was sure he didn't see where I was hiding, but he did.

He pulled right up to where I was hiding, so I jumped up to get away from him and that's when he exited his car and ran toward me. He lunged forward and pushed me across someone's front lawn. I could tell my foot was broken and he could tell he had gone too far. He ran and got back in his car and took off.

I got myself up and started to hobble down the street towards my house. Just then, a jeep pulls over and asks me if I need help and offers me a ride home. I have them take me to my street but not my house. I had to remove my high heels because I lived on a gravel road, so I walked to my house barefoot one slow agonizing step at a time. My foot was broken and bleeding from a laceration and dirt, dust and gravel from the road was getting into my cut. When I arrived at my house, my second son, the one who was addicted to pain pills, saw my foot and asked me what happened.

Without any explanation to him, I went straight to my room, changed my clothes and walked back out of the house. At that moment a neighbor drove by and asked if I wanted to come to their house. They lived to the right of my house further down our street. My house sat on this sharp curve of a dead-end road.

About an hour later one of their friends showed up and told us that the street was blocked off and they had to park one street over and walk down. They said there were ambulances and police at the house on the curve. I knew it was my house and the first thing that came to mind was that my son had stabbed my boyfriend. I don't know why; I just remember saying that to the neighbor, so they walked me home to see what was going on.

When the police allowed me in my house, I saw my house had been destroyed. I remember seeing a beer bottle had been thrown at my flat screen television in my bedroom. You could see the broken bottle lying on the floor under it and the splatter of the beer on the screen. All my belongings had been thrown across my room. This, however, was not the worse part. There was a trail of blood from my bedroom through the living room, all over the kitchen, hall and bathroom.

My boyfriend had come back to the house while I was at the neighbors and started destroying my room. My bedroom sits off the living room and you can also enter my bedroom from the side porch. My son heard the commotion and kicked my door in and confronted my boyfriend. They fought throughout the living room, kitchen, hall and bathroom. A knife was involved as my son tended to carry one. He has always felt some sense of responsibility in protecting me from a young age.

The ambulance treated my boyfriend for his injuries and then released him into the custody of the police. He was then taken to jail for the assault against me and my son was also arrested for the assault against my boyfriend. My son was released that night around midnight because he was a juvenile. The arresting officer brought him back home, which I was not expecting. He had just cut someone up and my house looked like the scene of a murder.

My boyfriend was denied bond for the domestic assault charge. He did have a record and was an adult. He sat in jail until he could get in front of a judge for a bond hearing. As the victim, I was served a subpoena to appear at the hearing. I cannot describe all the emotions a victim goes through. Everyone is different because we all have different situations.

There were moments when I felt like he needed to rot in jail and other moments where I excused his behavior and blamed the alcohol, myself, everything and anyone but him. I would rehearse what I would say to him the next time we spoke. Sometimes, it was how I was going to end it and other times I would rehearse asking him to quit drinking and that would make it all go away and I would feel safer knowing it would never happen again because it was the alcohols' fault. I was more afraid of being alone than being abused, even though I had been alone many times in my life. I was emotionally and physically tired of doing it all by myself.

We had only been dating a month or two, so I didn't have much invested in this relationship. There were decisions that needed to be made and I only had a few days to make them. The hearing was only a few days away and his fate lied in my hands. I could go in ready to testify and diminish his chances at getting a bond or I could notify the prosecution that I wanted them to lift the protection order and allow him a bond.

CHAPTER 3

CHANGES

My room was where I felt safe, it was dark, I had covered all the windows with heavy blankets because the blinds let too much light in. I was not ready to face the world or even see the sunlight. My kids helped put the house back together and clean all the blood that was splattered all over the house. We were doing our best to get back to normal, whatever that meant. There were a few casualties, like my flat screen television that never worked again after being hit with a beer bottle. Some broken picture frames and random knick knacks, all of which could be replaced.

I only have one commission check left in the pipeline and must find another place to live. I'm feeling overwhelmed with the pending court cases, for my son, my boyfriend, the case for overturning my judgment and my eviction had not been finalized, and my career in real estate was coming to an end. I knew I needed to make changes to support my family.

As I laid there in my room, depressed and stressed, healing my broken foot, taking pain medicine every four hours and watching a marathon of Dog the Bounty Hunter, I decided I was going to be a bail bond agent and fugitive recovery agent. I can't completely blame this idea on pain medicine, even though we all know they impair your judgment. I have always chosen risky careers. I have never worked an hourly or salary position. I believe that sets a limit to your income. I have always worked in sales, predominantly male industries like, floor covering and construction prior to my successful real estate career.

Some of this drive to be the bread winner stems from goals I set as a child. I grew up in and out of foster care for the first 10 years of my life and then spent a year at The East Tennessee Christian Home.

I remember I would stare at the sky as a child and wonder if my mother was staring at the same stars or clouds and at the same time as I. I knew my mother was under the same sky somewhere, we just didn't live under the same roof as normal families did. I prayed every day to be with my mother and I also made a lifelong goal for my unborn children that they will never have to look at the sky and wonder where I am. I didn't want them to feel what I felt. No matter how many jobs I would have to work, or the long hours it would take, I'll always be with them living under the same roof as it is supposed to be.

Two days later I was sitting in the court room and seeing a man I thought I loved, and I thought had loved me, dressed in an orange jumpsuit, handcuffed, hair is greasy from not getting a shower, arms are bandaged up from my son's assault, standing in front of the judge and all those in the court room, looking helpless. The whole situation gave me anxiety and as I sat there, I found myself feeling sorry for him. Disheartened, I just wanted to erase it all. My anger disappeared and my love and compassion took over, just as it had sporadically over the last few days. The longer I sat in the courtroom, conflicted as to what I should do, I heard the judge grant him a $10,000 bond. I got up to leave, which was a struggle with crutches, and I was approached by a bail bond agent who was willing to get him out.

All I had to do was come back around noon, pay the bond and sign some paperwork. The process seemed easy enough and her job even easier. I took a few moments to watch all the agents running around scrambling for business, as the agent approaching me had done. At this time, I had no knowledge of how illegal her actions or the other agents running around trying to get bonds was. It appeared to be an easy way to get business and business looked great. The courthouse was packed with potential clients.

This was my sign; this was my path, and this was what was going to save my family. I had made up my mind at that point that I was going to change my career. People were always going to go to jail. There will always be a need for bail bond agents, and it must be a business that is recession proof, unlike real estate. After going through the process of bonding him out of jail, I knew he wasn't the man I would marry one day and our time together would come to an end, and bail bonds would be my next big career and the only good thing to come from this tragic event.

CHAPTER 4

BECOMING AN AGENT

When I bonded my boyfriend out of jail, I asked the agent questions on how to become an agent. She did her best to make it sound harder than it was and to give as little information as possible. It was obvious as the nose on your face that she didn't want me to pursue my new career and get my license. From her reaction and responses to my questions along with what I had seen in the courthouse and at the jail, I could tell the business was very competitive. I think that aspect drew my interest even more.

I have always been the type of person to teach myself anyway, so I went online and researched how to become a bail bond agent in the state of Virginia. I learned that in the state of Virginia if you hold a bail bond license you also have the right to recover, meaning I didn't need a recovery license separate from my bail bond license to recover fugitives. However fugitive recovery agents cannot bail defendants out of jail.

Bail Bond Agent training consists of recovery training as well. There are two types of agents, property and surety agents in Virginia. I went for the surety license which means I had to also take the property and casualty insurance class and pass the state exam. I broke the steps down piece by piece and as I completed one process, I moved on to the next one. After getting all the information and signing up for my classes, I called around and told all my family and friends that I was going to become a bail bond agent. I was looking for support and encouragement, which I did not receive much of. Most of my family laughed and some of my friends looked forward to me receiving my license so I could help them out if needed. Most family members had seen me make decisions like this in the past and even though they laughed and made their jokes about this career choice, they knew if it was what I wanted to do, nothing was going to stop me and nothing did.

There are two types of bail bond agents, as I mentioned before, property and surety. Property agents use property valued at a minimum of $200,000 with no liens, to write bail against or have at least $200,000 in the bank to write against. You can write four times the amount of the value of your property or cash but could not exceed that amount at any given time. Some cases can take years to exonerate or finish. As a surety agent I had the ability to write billions, there was no limit of liability, and the sky was the limit, which is how I like it.

I received my license two months after I started the process, and I started in the business working for one of the lowest bail bond businesses around. I had no clue; he was the first one that returned my call, and I was ready to work. I thought I was working for a reputable business. Unfortunately, it didn't take long for me to realize that I accepted employment with one of the lowest bail bond companies in town. Unbelievably, everything I learned in school not to do; this guy was asking me to do.

I had about three weeks until the date I had agreed to move. The pressure was on me to make a huge amount of money in a short span of time. My boss, the slime ball, would ask me to solicit bail at bond hearings in the courthouse.

The same tactic that was done to me when I was a victim of domestic violence. I refused to do so. He would ask me to wear sexy shoes and clothes to the courthouse and invite male attorneys to lunch, which I also declined to do. I was a bail bond agent not a prostitute. I was not liking the vibe I was getting from him and the things he was asking me to do. I was uncomfortable with every interaction we had. His behavior was more like a pimp and not the owner of a legitimate bail bond business.

When I started my job, he gave me the phone lines for Stafford Jail which was about thirty-five minutes from my house with no traffic. None of his current agents wanted to work at that jail so the jail had been neglected for some time. All it took was for someone to answer the phone for the lines to start ringing off the hook. I worked day and night posting bail. There were days I was only home for an hour. Long enough to get a shower and if lucky a nap.

The hard work paid off and I got the money to move. The next morning, which was two days before I was supposed to be moving, the realtor I was working with called and said the owner, also an agent changed her mind about signing the lease.

I was devastated! I had been told three weeks prior that the new landlord had approved my application. I had informed the judge the day I wanted to move, and I had worked so hard to come up with all the money needed to move. I let him know we had nowhere else to go and he needed to do whatever was necessary to get me into that house.

I stared at my phone waiting for the call to come in. I was irritated every time it rang, and it wasn't my agent. A few hours later I got the call, she agreed to a six-month lease so I could prove myself and if all was good it would continue month to month. We all moved in, and my career was going well other than the fact I do not like who I was working for or his reputation.

I realized quickly that this was not the kind of reputation I wanted for myself. I wanted to do business differently and prove you can do business the right way and survive. Within three and a half months of learning what not to do, I opened Bad Girlz Bail Bonds LLC. This is where it all began....

CHAPTER 5

FRESH START

It was April 2011 and I've been licensed for a few months now and opened my own agency. I had my Jerry McGuire moment, only I was sitting in my car, and not in an office, and I was by myself, so nobody was coming with me. I was on my own and it was at that moment the name of my company was established and my slogan was born. I pulled over immediately to write it down because I tended to forget things.

I was ready to run my own agency. I was fed up with being asked to do things I was uncomfortable doing. My entire life always felt like one uncomfortable moment after another, this one I could control. I'm not a child being tossed around, I'm an adult in control of my own life. Up until this point in my career, I had not done any fugitive recovery while working for the other company. My only experience in the business was posting bail.

I knew how to market my business; I had been successful in the past in marketing myself in real estate. I was confident in my ability to build this business. New ads for the jails wouldn't hit until July. This meant my phone numbers wouldn't be in the jail for three months. This was a slight setback; all my business would have to be referral because my number would not be listed in intake. I would have to market in other unconventional ways for a few months to get my name out there and I would need to keep my business above water until July.

This was a pivotal moment in my career. I wasn't going to do business as other companies were. I couldn't bring myself to solicit at the bail hearings or at the jails, as was done to me, although it was nice to get the process over quickly and efficiently it was illegal.

I was going to build my business on who I am and the service I can provide. I had just started my first personal social media account while I was getting my license to help reconnect with people. Once I opened my business, I built a business page and started to promote my page everywhere I went.

I didn't know much about social media, and I always disliked computers. I had a blackberry when they first came out and only used it to make phone calls. I had no idea the things that phone could do, and it could have made my life much simpler had I known how to use it.

The business page grew, and my phone rang enough to keep the lights on, food on the table, and pay the rent. I didn't know at the time how beneficial this page would become. In my mind I was building a page to get people out of jail. My business page became instrumental in not only getting calls for bail, but it also became beneficial in catching some of the most dangerous criminals I've ever encountered. On my page I shared my life experiences and struggles with my son's addiction and my past addiction. I was transparent and real, sometimes to a fault.

I shared the good, the bad, and the funny stories and always did my best to be a woman of my word. The first few months were the hardest. The competition wasn't very welcoming to another company opening. The previous company I had worked for tried to embed in me that competition was the enemy.

The competition was fierce at times, we all had to eat, and all had families to support. Was being enemies the answer though? Wouldn't we all do better if we worked together to help one another out? I had a different approach. I would call the other agents every morning and say good morning and see how they were doing. I got their numbers from their ads, none of them had ever offered up their number to me at this point. Some agents were taken back by me calling them and seeing if they were good. It's not something they were used to, that's for sure.

Usually if you're calling the competitor, it was to yell at them about stealing a bond and not to see how they are doing. When we were all sitting at the jail serving our time (as we called it) on the other side waiting for paperwork, I would always try and lighten the mood in the lobby. After all no one is happy about sitting in jail, no matter which side you're on.

There were no comforts in the bonding lobby, no TV, no vending machines, just a room with a teller window to slide paperwork back and forth to the magistrate and a bathroom. There were also only six chairs and one table, and the lobby could fill up quickly, so the agents spent most of the time standing or pacing.

You could be in the lobby posting bail all day for different clients or stuck there for hours on end for a bond with an error in the court file. We spent a lot of time together whether it's what we wanted or not. I figure it was best we all got along. I could never win the friendships of everyone and that was ok with me. Not everyone was my cup of tea either. I can get along with most people, I only have a problem with the rude, the arrogant, and the mean people.

In the beginning it almost felt like being back in school. The drama between agents and the talking behind each other's backs. I knew I wasn't immune to the same type of behavior when I wasn't present. I knew who the ones were that would smile in my face, and when I wasn't around, they would make bets with other agents on how long I would survive in the business. They were hoping I would post a large bond and lose the fugitive and go out of business.

My ads finally hit, and my number is now in intake and my business has survived. My marketing was different from all the other ads. It caught the eye of everyone! The corrections officers, the other agents and most importantly the defendants sitting in intake trying to get bonded out.

I tried to be creative, I had hired a tattoo artist to draw a cartoon of a bad girl holding a key. The background was the jail with the inmate being released with an attorney by his side and I had a great slogan, "When Bad Girlz hold the key, you're as good as free!" My phone started ringing off the hook. I was finally their competition, their equal. The playing field had been leveled and I felt great!

Some of the competitors could not stop talking about my ad in the lobby. My name was being talked about repeatedly and some agents had a habit of bringing up my Facebook page as they were making fun of my company. It only drove their clients to my page to see what it was all about, which in turn grew my page. Bad publicity is still publicity, and they were slowly but surely building my business right along with me.

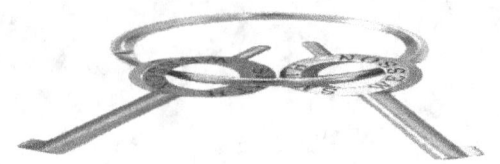

CHAPTER 6

FIRST RESPONDERS

    Six months in and business was going well. I had made some friendships within the business and even gained a mentor. My mentor said to me early on "Carol, we are first responders. People don't get arrested because everything is going great with their lives. Something is going on and we are the first people there to speak to them. Make it count." That really stuck with me my entire career. Here I am, bonding addicts, alcoholics, homeless and mentally ill people out of jail.

What service was I providing, other than letting them out of jail to continue their path of self-destruction for a fee? I was benefiting from their call, but how were they benefiting from calling me? Was I doing all I could? Did I say what needed to be said to someone to change their life in a positive way? I had to be more to my clients than the person getting them out for a fee. I was committed to being a first responder and trying to make a positive change in as many lives as was possible.

I talked to many parents, spouses, siblings and loved ones at the jail from many walks of life, sometimes for hours on end and could relate to them through my own life experiences. I could have, and almost did ruin my life with drugs. I made different choices and pulled myself out. Some would say I did it before it was too late, I would say it's never too late if you're still upright and breathing, you can make changes. I used my time wisely at the jail to not only build my business but to build relationships with people in hopes of helping them to a better path. One that doesn't lead them in and out of jail or into a cemetery. I made it a point to tell every client, whether addiction, abuse or any other issues arise, no matter the time of day or night, if their loved one started using, abusing someone, become a danger to themselves or the community by committing more crimes I would pick them up for free and place them back in jail.

I then made sure to let every defendant know when they walked out of jail, any issues whatsoever, I'm picking you up and putting you back and it won't cost your signer a dime. We are not doing anyone a favor by keeping someone on the street who is a danger to themselves or the community. If I can prevent you from getting more charges, hurting someone or killing yourself by revoking your bond, I will choose to do so every time.

Most bail bond agents would charge to revoke bonds and I understand it from a business point of view. However, I felt more inclined to change and save lives and knew I would get what was needed to provide for my family. God has always made a way for me and though I have struggled, I was never alone, and those times have made me the woman I am today, and I would not change it.

CHAPTER 7

NO TWO DAYS THE SAME

When I started Bad Girlz Bail, I depended on me and me alone. If it failed, it was me, there was no one else to blame. I had owned other businesses, however I depended on subcontractors to install the work I would sell. When they get paid you may not see them for a few days. When you have jobs scheduled and no installers, you try and call your client and make excuses in hopes you don't lose the job. You depend on others to run a business; this was going to be different because I only needed me for the most part. I knew my work ethic, so this didn't worry me at all. I ran day and night and answered every call.

I worked most holidays due to the phone ringing more than usual because no other company was answering their phones. There are no set hours, people get arrested at all hours of the day. You are on call 24 hours a day 7 days a week. In bail, you are either waiting on the next bail call or the tip that leads you to a fugitive you have been hunting down. Making plans with friends or family was impossible, unless you could afford to miss a call, which I could not.

When building my business and being the bread winner for my family of five, I couldn't afford to miss a thing. I did love my job; I never knew where my office was for the day. I could be spending my day posting bail in the jails, staking out a trap house, or driving across the country on a hunt for someone who failed to appear. You never knew when you were going to sleep or shower so you took naps and showers when possible.

Some days I would reach my driveway only to receive another call for bail and need to turn around and go right back to where I had just come from. This could happen several times in a day. Business was good, I had no reason to complain. My company grew both on social media and throughout the jail. I was getting referrals from past clients and had some repeat clients.

I was never the 9-5 office type of person. I didn't like having to show up at the same place every day and stay there for hours on end. That felt like a jail sentence to me and not a job. Like ground hog day the movie, the same thing over and over. There were other women in the business, but it was a predominantly male business. Most women in the business were in business with their spouses and usually, their husbands would handle the fugitive recovery.

There were a few women that worked for various companies however they were posting agents holding zero liability. They did not do fugitive recovery; they did not care if the defendant was going to appear. They posted bail for a fee and the company they worked for would do the recovery. I was responsible for every dime I wrote. If someone failed to appear, it was on me. Being a single mother of four, I didn't have money in the bank to pay those bonds. I rented my home and barely got that. I drove an old car that had a title loan and had to hide it from time to time and barely made ends meet month to month. The liability for every bond is supposed to lie with the signer. When I post bail, a family member or friend sign responsibility for the defendant's appearance in court and if they fail to appear, the signer owes Bad Girlz Bail the full amount of the bond.

Most of these families could barely afford the bond premium, much less the whole bond. I could take them to court, which cost me time and money and it can take months to get into court and receive a judgement. We all know a judgement doesn't pay the bond. There were times in the beginning where I would post a risky bond for practice.

You just knew the bonds you would have an issue with. Usually, the first sign is when the family close to them doesn't want to get them out and they have a friend bonding them out. Often, if your family doesn't want you out, there is an issue. Another sign would be if they lived out of state. I would decide those based on if it was a state I'd like to visit. There were times when things would be going on in my personal life and I was more comfortable in the county jail. Times when I needed to keep my mind occupied and those were when I wrote the riskiest bonds.

There were very few happy endings in bail, but there were some and those were the cases I lived for. For me it was time to step up to the plate. Be a woman of my word. This was my business, my money, my life and the lives of others depended on me doing my job to the best of my ability. Knowing when to say no to a bond and knowing when to pick someone up.

The next learning curve of my career was about to begin. It was time to revoke bonds as needed to save lives and recover fugitives as needed to save money. It was time to go to work and hopefully make a positive impact on others.

CHAPTER 8

MY FIRST REVOCATION

I know how difficult it is to put your child in jail. However, at the time of this revocation I had no idea. Later in my career I became known as the agent who recovered her own son. A case I will discuss further in the future.

My first recovery was not my son, but rather a young girl addicted to heroin. She was around the same age as my son. She told the same lies at the jail that I have heard from my son. She had this zombie like appearance as most who used heroin did.

If you have never experienced a loved one addicted to heroin, you are truly blessed. It is difficult to watch someone's life dwindle away. The suffering in between getting high almost makes you want to put them out of their own misery at times. It's almost like watching an animal suffer that's been hit by a car.

The battle is within themselves and unfortunate to the ones that love them, you cannot save them. They must save themselves. Something that took me years to learn and to this day I'm still not comfortable with putting that responsibility in my son's own hands.

The day started as any other day. I woke around 3:30 a.m. to grab a shower before the phone started ringing. I spent the entire day running back and forth between two jails and returned home around 11:30 p.m. I was getting ready for bed when I got a notification from my business page of a message. I was so tired and really wanted to avoid the message until the morning, but my curiosity wouldn't allow it. I know curiosity killed the cat. I grabbed my phone and prepared myself to get out of bed. I had had only three to four hours sleep the night before and I was burning both ends of the candle.

The message was from one of my clients and I could feel her desperation and anxiety when reading her message. Her daughter had been running the streets for days using heroin again and just returned home. She tells me she is on the living room couch sleeping and would like me to come to the house and take her back to jail.

This was the first call I had received to revoke a bond. I had no one to call for help, it was in the middle of the night, and I had offered to pick her up free of charge if something like this happened. Bringing another agent in would mean I would have to pay them. I didn't have the extra money to do that. I had to do this on my own. I got up and printed the paperwork I needed to pick her up. I had to take it to the magistrate's office to get the bail piece signed in order to legally revoke her bond and arrest her. After getting everything in order I then headed over to my client's home.

The thing about addiction is it spares no one. I pulled up to this beautiful three-story brick colonial with the three-car garage, fully covered front porch with a swing and a privacy fence surrounding their inground pool. At this point I realized addiction is a nationwide issue affecting everyone, it doesn't just prey on a certain race or income bracket.

I sent the mother a message that I was there and to come, open the door quietly and let me in. The mother said she wanted to talk to me first and told me she was going to step outside. She came to the porch and first apologized to me for calling me out so late. It is about 2:00 a.m. at this point; I haven't seen my bed since 3:30 a.m. the morning before. She continues to tell me she had changed her mind. She wanted to try and get her to agree to go to rehabilitation the next day.

I was trying to understand her feelings and at the same time save her child. I had gotten out of bed, as soon as I got in it, drove to the jail to see the magistrate and put this effort into saving her child because she got me involved. I couldn't walk away knowing she wasn't in rehabilitation or jail and away from the drugs. I'm here now and I must know this girl is safe.

After talking with mom, we came to an agreement. We were going to let her daughter decide her fate. The plan was to wake her up, I would put her in custody, and we would give her a choice, rehabilitation or jail but it was happening right then, not the next day. They never go the next day and sometimes the next day is too late. We went into the house, and we woke her up.

I put her in cuffs before she realized what had happened and explained to her that I was there to take her back to jail as I had promised I would do if she continued to use heroin. I had to be stern and let her know I mean business.

She was a mess, wearing only a dirty white tank top and some gym shorts. I could see needle marks throughout her arms, neck, the back of her knees and between her fingers. The same places I would see them on my own son. She looked like she hadn't showered or eaten in days. Her lips looked cracked from dehydration and her skin was a pale complexion with dark circles and bags around her eyes.

She was calm at first and played the victim well, claiming she hadn't been using drugs and all the marks were old. Her tears ran down her face telling her mom if I let her go, she will go to rehabilitation tomorrow. Mom was starting to crack so I had to remind mom of our deal and let her know her daughter was leaving with me to go to rehabilitation or jail.

I'm a mom and I wanted to crack as well but I knew I couldn't. I had to be the strength her mom wasn't possessing at that time. I can't tell you how nice it would have been to see someone standing next to me fighting for my son. I didn't have that; I couldn't even rely on his father's help, much less anyone else.

When our son became an addict, he washed his hands clean of him. There were times I envied him for being able to walk away, those were very weak moments. I just wondered what it's like to not give a shit. To walk around without a care in the world. If I could feel that way maybe I wouldn't walk around so stressed and on edge. Always waiting for the call that my son took it too far and overdosed. I didn't want the stress, aggravation, frustration, and worry watching my child kill themself, but I didn't have a choice like he apparently did.

I couldn't leave my sons side and I couldn't be the person I was being for this woman to my own child. The defendant had a choice, rehabilitation or jail. She decided to try and fight a little in cuffs and begged her mother to change her mind. She didn't realize mom wasn't the one in control here.

I held the keys and the paperwork for her future. The fighting didn't work in her favor and at this point she is starting to see me go from concerned too angry. I wanted to get her in a safe pace and maybe get an hour or so sleep before the bond calls start coming in. The mother was crying and getting upset, making it even harder for me to take control of the situation.

I needed her support and for her daughter to see her mother was doing this to save her and that we were a united front. Showing weakness at this point in the game was not going to benefit her daughter. I knew I needed to get control and the only way to do that was to go ahead and remove her from the house and separate mom and daughter. After gaining control of her daughter and as I was taking her out of the house, the mother right on my tail, begging me to leave her there.

I once again reiterated our deal and let her know I refused to leave her daughter on my bond knowing she was using drugs and could die at any moment. I won't be one of those agents turning death certificates into the court to get off a bond. I let her mom know she would be back at the jail, and she could bond her out again through another company if that's what she chooses to do.

My advice to mom was to let her sit until she gets her head right and gets the drugs out of her system. Then I would only bond her under the condition she goes straight from jail to rehabilitation.

In the car on the way to the jail I tried to talk to her and get to know why she was throwing her life away. She had mentioned some issues she had with her mother and blamed her mother for her addiction and didn't want her mother around her. She claimed that's why she left the house for days. She then proceeded to get angrier the closer we got to the jail. She started to cuss at me for the rest of the ride as if that was going to help her and let me know she would warn everyone in jail not to use my company for bail. I let her know that I am doing my part to help save her life. I knew she didn't see it then but hopefully one day when her mind was clear, she would. I never heard from her or her mother again. I did see she was bailed out of jail by the next morning. I can only hope and pray she turned her life around.

CHAPTER 9

THE INCEST CASE

It was about three weeks before Christmas, and the weather had changed to cold and the lobby at the jail would be frigid for the next few months. The jail didn't like to pay for heat, and people would walk in and out constantly letting the little heat we did have out of the door. The bonding lobby was treated no differently than the cells in the back. I have been in the business a year and have made several recoveries with our agents and they have helped me with a few of mine. I was enjoying recovery work and the adrenaline rush it gave me.

I accepted every opportunity to join other agents on their cases for the experience and to prove myself worthy as a recovery agent. There was nothing unusual about this call. A twenty-two-year-old girl trying to bond her dad out of jail. Sometimes the kids have their lives together and are the ones getting the parents out of jail, as was the case here.

I had worked out a payment plan because she didn't have all the premium. The down payment didn't even cover my cost to write the bond and as with any payment plan, you never know if you will see another dime. I just wanted to make sure she had her dad home for Christmas. I met the daughter at the jail and started the paperwork with the authorities there to get him released while she was filling out her paperwork to accept responsibility for the bond. This is a prime example of a signer not being able to cover the bond if they fail to appear. I was aware of the risk but confident if there was an issue, I would be able to handle it.

She didn't speak much, only when spoken to and she would reply with short answers. The lobby was empty, it was just her and I, so the paperwork came through quicker than normal, and he was released.

He walked through the release door, which sends the inmates outside, it's where I wait after signing the bond, so they don't slip by without doing their paperwork and getting their photo taken, and we walked into the lobby to do his paperwork.

When my client saw her dad, she ran up to him and hugged him for like five minutes. She then reached up and placed her hand on his neck and gave him a kiss on the side of his neck. At this point I'm questioning if I misunderstood their relationship. The greeting felt more like one with a sexual nature. I look over the paperwork and it's right there in black and white, relationship to defendant, daughter.

I don't know the situation and I never like to assume. I have no clue how she was raised and maybe that's how it's supposed to be. I wouldn't know, my dad was not in my life much at all. We have met a few times throughout my adult life and spoken over text some. I have no childhood memories with my dad. What do I know about father daughter relationships? It was kind of a slow day, so I packed up my stuff and headed home, hoping to get some housework done and maybe a nap. You take advantage of all the down time to handle personal business like your bills, housework and grocery shopping.

A few weeks have gone by, and it has been business as usual. Christmas is three days away and everyone is in the spirit of Christmas. Agents are filling the lobby releasing people, and families are being reunited with loved ones before the Christmas holiday. It was like a marathon, working day and night trying to help as many people as we could, and every company was on board. We were all pulling sixteen to eighteen-hour days.

I'm sitting at the jail posting bail and I receive a call from a woman claiming to be the aunt to the girl who bonded her dad out of jail a few weeks earlier. She tells me that her niece just met her dad within the last six months. She explains her niece has some mental issues and has fallen in love with her dad and he with her.

She continues to tell me that the niece and the dad are in a relationship. It all clicks at that moment. I may not have had a dad in my life, but I knew that wasn't appropriate behavior. Having a dad or not I had never seen someone kiss their dad like that. Her aunt confides in me the struggle the family is having trying to get her away from him and in getting her some help for her mental illness.

She asks me if she is willing to set him up, would I be willing to pick him up and revoke the bond? She didn't have to ask me twice, I agreed to revoke the bond and we set it up for later that evening. I got as much information as I could regarding her vehicle description and where I needed him to be sitting in the vehicle. I also needed to know who all would be in the vehicle and that there were no weapons.

I started getting my paperwork together and realized he was a fugitive and he had failed to appear on my bond just three days earlier, I just hadn't received my show cause, which at times could take weeks depending on the jurisdiction. I also never received another dime from him or his daughter towards the premium they owed me. In doing my paperwork I found out he was also wanted out of another county for another failure to appear.

I wasn't going alone on this one. I had two guys straight out of Fugitive Recovery class that wanted to ride along. They found me on my Facebook page and contacted me for business. I wasn't comfortable working with agents with zero experience but then I remember, I once stood where these guys do now. This recovery shouldn't be an issue being its being set up and they in return will gain some experience.

I get everything set up to meet at a gas station off interstate 95 in Caroline County. We arrived about forty-five minutes early so we could get our plan together on how we were going to take him down. Where we would be parked and where we needed the CI to park in order to grab him quickly.

When we pulled in the parking lot, there were two state troopers and two county police cars in the parking lot. I remember thinking of all the places to meet we chose a police meeting spot; this can't be good. The Aunt had no Idea he was a fugitive, but he did, and he was probably going to stop her from stopping there once he sees their cars in the parking lot. If I was a fugitive, the last place I'm going to is a gas station with four cop cars.

I decided to go in and talk to the police and let them know what was about to go down and asked them how long they would be in the gas station. I know this sounds ironic, but they were in the station drinking coffee and eating donuts. It had apparently been a slow evening. The State Troopers left within a few minutes, but the two county cars asked if they could hang around and watch. I agreed when I got the call, they would go across the street to McDonald's. The officers pulled up next to my vehicle and we kind of compared notes on apprehensions.

They tell me that they follow me on my Bad Girlz page and love my post. I'll never forget this officer asking me if I ran after people if they ran from me. I told him I wasn't a big fan of cardio and that's why I carry a taser. By the size of him I could tell he was also not a big fan of cardio. The county he worked in was a very small county where everyone knew everyone. He had his regulars as I did.

It was getting close to go time, so the officers headed across the street to McDonalds. My heart is racing, this is what I live for. The adrenaline when you catch someone you've been looking for is far better than any street drug. I don't think I slept for two days after my very first recovery. I was a little more nervous on this one because not only did I have two rookies with me, but I also had police spectators. I didn't want to make any mistakes when we were in a public location with innocent bystanders all around us. I had to make sure all were protected.

About five minutes later the call we had been waiting for came in. They were five minutes out and suddenly changed their mind. They're going to McDonalds across the street.

There is no way I can tell the cops the location changed to where they have moved to; they're already sitting in the McDonald's parking lot, so we had to do this quick. I texted her where to park and we headed across the street to where I could easily pull up behind them and block their vehicle as they parked. She pulls in the parking lot, and I get in behind her. As she parks her vehicle, we block her in, and I jump out of the passenger side of my vehicle. I had to move fast and get him before he knew what hit him. The police were in clear view and were waiting to make sure I had no issues.

I ran up to the back passenger door, pulled it open and grabbed the defendant by his shoulders and yanked him out of the back seat and took him to the ground. By this time the two agents were right there assisting me as I'm placing him in cuffs. After securing him, we stand him up and search him for any contraband, drugs, weapons and any items that are not allowed in the jail.

I don't generally like to see fugitives get new charges; they have enough problems. I usually explain to someone why their bond is being revoked but he had already failed to appear, and this was a recovery not a revocation; he was a fugitive, and no explanation was needed.

There were times you would find pocketknives or a dime bag of weed while searching a recovery, these are the types of things I can destroy and overlook. However, if they're carrying an amount that is at a distribution level, like the fifty bags of heroin I found on one fugitive I caught, the police will get called to the scene and they're getting more charges.

After I cleared him, his daughter asked if she could say goodbye and she got out of the car and ran up to him and did the same thing she did at the jail. She grabbed his neck and kissed him on the neck. The two county cops pulled their cars over once we had him in cuffs and stood back out of the way until all was clear. They approached me and asked if they could take him in. They had already told me they don't see much action in their county, and they were bored and had nothing going on.

I agreed to let them take him, I had them sign my paperwork, we switched the handcuffs on him, and they took custody of him. I was happy to hand him over. The drive to jail with a fugitive can be very unpleasant. Some fugitives will fight the entire way, some will try and open the door and jump out.

I have gotten the angry, the sick and the apologetic ones, the ones that tell you they weren't running yet they aren't responding to any form of communication and when you catch them, they tell you they were going to turn themselves in.

I did my best to stay prepared for all these possibilities with every recovery. Always search the fugitive prior to putting them in the vehicle, sometimes twice, child safety locks on all the time, never place a fugitive in the front seat or behind a driver, always have an agent sitting in the back with the fugitive and always cuff in the back. These are just a few examples of my safety protocol when transporting a fugitive.

I have had fugitives contact me when they finish serving their time and thank me for picking them up. Some have offered their services like tattooing, I respectfully decline. I don't know about letting someone tattoo you that you picked up off the street and put in jail. The dad stayed in jail for some time and never called my company again for bail. He knew better I suppose, he didn't pay his bail payments and he didn't go to court. The daughter was placed in a hospital and was receiving treatment.

The aunt called me several times to thank me and update me on her progress and then the communication just stopped. My job isn't always about reaching the defendants. My client is not the defendant as most people would think. My client is the signer, the person signing the paperwork at the jail, the third party to the bond, that takes the liability for the full amount of the bond plus recovery fees. I'm aware that reaching a defendant in a way that changes their life will also improve the life of my client, the loved one bonding them out. In this case my client was being abused and we removed the abuser. This case will always be in my memory, and I will always wonder what she made of her life.

I did work with the "rookie" agents on a few more cases until they parted and moved away. They did a great job having my back, we had one under and we all went home safe. That always makes for a great day!

CHAPTER 10

DOUBLE CROSS

I was the sole agent for my company Bad Girlz Bail Bonds LLC. I had been in business about a year at this time and had made partnerships on recoveries with other agents. I help them, they help me, we all save money. I had asked this one agent if he would help me grab a fugitive that recently failed to appear. Even though I was reluctant to work with this guy, we all could see something was going on with him in his personal life. I thought maybe working together I could get some answers as to what was going on with him and maybe help him out.

He agreed to help me, so we met up at Hardees about a mile from the gated apartment complex where my fugitive was living. He tells me we are going to eat first. I was thinking dear lord let's just go get this guy. I don't like wasting time especially after I get a lead. After looking at the agent he looked like he needed to eat so we went inside and got breakfast and discussed the case.

It was early in the day, about 8:00 a.m. I remember it was a grey cloudy day and it was wet from drizzle almost like a mist. All women know this makes for a bad hair day. I however wasn't worried about my hair, I just wanted to get this guy and get on with my day doing something that was going to pay the bills, like post bail.

We ate breakfast then got into his vehicle leaving mine at Hardees, and then headed to the apartment complex. As soon as we pulled up another car came through the gate, so we took our shot and drove through while it was open. My heart starts to race a little as it always does before a recovery. My palms were sweaty, and I was feeling nervous working with this guy, I could tell something was off with him.

I had never worked with this agent, so I didn't know what to expect from him. He had been in the business longer than me so he should be well trained, but he is acting a little nervous himself. At times during the ride over he was covered in sweat, and I was sure he had nodded out at a streetlight. My second thought was maybe he was up all-night posting bail and was just tired.

We pulled up to the apartment building and there he was. My fugitive, his girlfriend the signer, and their newborn baby in a baby carrier walking out to their car. I wanted to pull behind them to block him in and take them down, right there. Seemed like the best thing to do. He has a baby, is he really going to want to put that child in danger? I thought it was our best shot at a quick take down, but the other agent allows them to back out and drive away.

At this point I'm pretty sure this agent is going to mess this up. I don't know what he is thinking, we had a great opportunity to get him as soon as they got in their car. I am not happy at all with the way he is doing things and not sure I can trust this guy with my life. He is acting reckless and I'm about to call it off even though my fugitive is in sight. It's my job to make it home every day for my kids.

It's not my job to pull stupid stunts that can endanger myself, the other agent or innocent bystanders. We got in behind him leaving some distance so we wouldn't be noticed. Now we are following this fugitive, having no clue where we are going. I don't like it; I like to control my environment when doing recovery as much as possible.

I'm kind of a control freak. I won't fly in planes because I'm not the one in control. They pulled into a medical center, and we blocked their car in there. How in the world is this any safer than the apartment complex? The apartment complex had less people around to possibly endanger. No one was in the apartment complex parking lot when we pulled up other than the fugitive and his family.

I get out of the car and I'm at the passenger door within seconds. The other agent was still sitting in the car when he should have been right behind me, and he appeared to be nodding out again. I yelled at him to get out of the car and assist. I have no weapon and I can see him reaching for something in the car. He locks his door his window is rolled up; His girlfriend knew it was over and I could tell she was telling him something, but I couldn't hear the conversation. I'm sure whatever it was, it was to protect the baby in the back seat. The other agent was carrying a firearm and he is two times my size and he is sitting in the car nodding off and putting my life in danger. I yell over at him again, as I'm blocking the fugitive from exiting the car, and he wakes up and walks up behind me and assists me with getting this man out of the car.

We got him secure, and I asked the other agent to perform a search on him and place him in the back. Male agents search male defendants and female search female, another golden rule. I had to sit in the back with the fugitive and on the way to the jail the fugitive keeps saying, he could stab me, he could kill me, over and over. I ignored his shit talking and we finally arrived at the jail which was only about twenty minutes from where we apprehended him, however it felt like much longer. The other agent took him out of the car and had a conversation with the fugitive at the back of the car that I could not make out, but I could tell by their body language, they were up to something.

I take the fugitive by the arm and walk him into intake. The corrections officer takes the paperwork, and they proceed to do their search and switch cuffs. When performing a search on him, the officer finds a knife with a five-inch blade on the fugitive.

I'm angry now, I'm realizing my life was in the hands of a clown. How in the hell did that agent miss that? What was he saying at the back of the car and was he aware that this fugitive that I was sitting next to in the backseat was armed? Whose side was this guy on? Looking back, I almost felt as though I was the one being set up.

The officers called the county officers, and the fugitive received another charge. I never worked with that agent again. I did hear from him about six months later. He called me from a jail in Northern Virginia, he had caught some drug charges. I refused to help him and never heard from him again. I heard through other agents he was bonded out and took off to West Virginia.

He had property in West Virginia, from an inheritance and had always talked about going there. I was glad he wasn't my problem; I didn't bond him out. It was sad to see him throw his life away to drugs. I do have compassion for him in that sense. He lost everything from his license to do business, which cost him his livelihood which in turn made him lose everything he had, many friends, his car and his home in Virginia.

I realized after that encounter; it was time for me to add an agent to my agency. Someone I can trust and depend on when other agents aren't available.

CHAPTER 11

BUS DRIVER

I'm sitting in my room; the phone has been quiet so I'm relaxing, and my son enters the room. He asks me if I could help this lady he knows, who was a bus driver, get her husband out of jail. I have mentioned my son's addiction and some of my personal struggles in dealing with it. Anyone he wants bonded out of jail, I want to know who they are and where they live. I was the type of mother who would post a huge note on your front door, asking you to stop selling heroin to my son in big bold letters, if I knew you were selling to my son. My son became addicted at the age of fourteen to pain medicine.

He had a kidney stone removed surgically and the doctor prescribed him oxycontin. He then started buying pills off the street and moved on to heroin because it was cheaper. I had heard rumors of a bus drivers' husband that would sell pills to the kids, but they were only rumors. I had to get the information from my son about this bus driver and her husband, so I at least had them on my radar. He gave me the bus driver's number and I called her and agreed to meet her at the jail.

In my mind, if he is selling to my kid, it's best he is on my bond, where I can throw him back if needed. I also wanted to talk to this woman and find out how she knows my son. It didn't take long for all the pieces of the puzzle to come together. I bonded him out and within a few weeks they had pissed my son off. He came home asking me to revoke his bond. The way my son was acting, I could tell this was a drug deal gone wrong and knew I had bonded one of his many suppliers. I refused my son's request. He does not control my business; he never has, and I'll be damned if I'll allow it now. He is not my signer so he damn sure wasn't my client. A few weeks go by, and a sheriff comes to my door with a show cause. I was walking out to go to the jail and post a bond as he was walking up. We exchange our pleasantries as we always had done, and he hands me the show cause and says the defendant's name.

I was totally floored! The bus driver's husband failed to appear! I walked back into my house and up to my office and printed my bail piece; I was headed to the jail already so best to get this out of the way so I'm prepared to grab him when I can. I posted his fugitive status on my business page and went about my day.

Three days go by, and I haven't heard anything regarding my fugitive. I called the signer, and she claimed they're no longer together. I don't believe it for one second. I believe she is just as much of a dealer as he is. I believe she preyed upon the high schoolers she drove to school and provided clients for her husband. If I could have locked her up, I would have.

I posted him up again as a fugitive and while I was sitting in Stafford jail, I got a lead on my page. It came in around 9:30 p.m. I needed to finish my bond and try and get some agents together, before I could check it out. I looked the address up and realized it was about two miles from my home and only seven miles to the jail.

I called several agents in the area; some were already in bed by the time I finished my bond or sitting in a jail. I decided I'm just going to drive by on the house and check out the area. The house was in a rural part of the county, on a small country road with no streetlights. It was pitch black outside. No outside lights were on, but there were lights on inside the home. I don't know what came over me, I just decided to park my car and go to the door.

I beat on the door and yelled "department of criminal justice". A young man comes to the door, and I tell him who I am and who I am there for. I also tell him that I have his house surrounded and so he can either send him out or we're coming in. He shuts the door and I hear him say "you got to go man!" The front door opens again, and the man threw my fugitive out on the front porch followed by his shoes and shuts the door. I get him in cuffs and help him put his shoes on. We proceed to my vehicle where I secure him in the backseat and then walk around to the driver's side. As I'm putting my seatbelt on, he says to me "hey, where is your team at?" I said, "you see it." He replied, "you said the house was surrounded". I replied, "I lied, like you did when you said you would go to court."

He was quiet the rest of the ride to jail, which was good because I was nervous about riding in the car without another agent and I didn't want him to see it. You never want to show fear no matter how scared you are.

He tried several times to get me to post bail for him again over the years and was denied every time. I wouldn't be of service to him to continue to bond him out so he could rack up more charges. Sometimes it's best to let them sit, it does wonders for their criminal record when they cannot be on the streets reoffending.

CHAPTER 12

MEGAN

    I had decided it was time to hire an agent. I had many people contact me over my first year asking if I was hiring. You learn, be careful who you hire or you could be training your next competitor. I needed someone that I could count on to have my back and wouldn't leave me after training. What better person than one of my best friends. I met Megan when she came to my daughter's birthday party in 2009 with a mutual friend of ours. We hit it off and started to hang out almost immediately. Megan liked to frequent a bar about a mile from her house. This bar had poker tournaments every night of the week. I wasn't a drinker and was there for the poker.

Megan liked to sit at the bar and mingle, she knew everyone and all their business. Fast forward to 2012, Megan met the love of her life and settled down. No longer spending her nights at the local bar. We hadn't been hanging out much, me with my new career and always on call and her with her new man.

She was struggling with her current career, and I needed help, so I asked her if she wanted to become an agent. Her husband was diagnosed with cancer, and I could offer her a schedule that catered to his appointments. She can write bail when she is available and be paid full-time wages for part-time work.

She was excited for the opportunity, so I walked her through the process. She completed the classes and received her license in about two months' time. I started to train her on posting bail, taking her to the jails with me to post bonds. Showing her how to do the signer, defendant and jail paperwork. Making sure she had the process down before letting her loose on her own. When we got past that training, she was ready for recovery training. One thing I knew about Megan, she was good at finding information about anyone. She was the 9-5 office type, so she loved doing research on the computer whereas I loved the work in the field.

She wasn't chosen for her stature, standing about five foot six inches tall and weighing in at about a hundred and twenty pounds. She was not intimidating, she was the exact opposite, which was needed in some cases. We played off each other well and had very creative ways of catching fugitives as you will read in this book. She had an innocent look to her whereas I came off a little harder. We made a great team.

Photo Credit Tre Hoover

Cat pictured on the right and Megan on the left

CHAPTER 13

ROOKIE MISTAKE

It's been a few months since my best friend started working for me. We were like two peas in a pod, if the pod had one green pea and one any other color of the rainbow, almost like twins. We had creative ways of catching fugitives and were getting noticed by other agencies all over the country. Megan and I had been out to dinner, it was mid-summer, so we were eating on the patio making plans to get into something when the phone rang. It was a call from the jail right down the street from where we were eating.

So, we decided to entertain it and answer the phone. We could make some quick money and then find something to do. I had dealt with this guy earlier in the day. He had called me, another inmate, who referred people to me all the time, assured me the guy was good. I went to the jail to get him out and had a bad feeling, so I changed my mind and pulled the card and left. This kid was about twenty-two years old and had a $5000 bond. He said he had all the cash at his house and his grandparents would sign if I took him there. I knew this was a terrible bond and wanted nothing to do with it, however Megan talks me into pulling him out.

Boredom always got us in trouble. As was the case here, we had nothing to do, the phones were quiet so we made the decision knowing it was risky and could possibly turn out bad. We agreed we were going to bond him, and he would stay in our custody while we took him to his house to get the money and have his grandparents sign the bail paperwork. We arrive at the jail, and we post the bond to get this kid out. I must admit he looked innocent enough and he did remind me of one of my sons. No harm could possibly come from this.

We had him fill out his paperwork at the jail, took his photo and cuffed him. This is where the rookie mistake happened. I'm going to cuff him with his hands behind his back and Megan said, "Carol, we can cuff him in the front he isn't going to do anything." Now, I have more experience and know this is a bad idea but hey, everyone must learn somehow and if need be, I could take this kid. We walk him out and make sure he is fully secured in the car. He starts to act nervous, and I knew at that moment he had gotten us. Megan was also about to learn a lesson that she will never forget as well. I'm watching every move he makes, every expression on his face and every bead of sweat falling off his forehead. I started lacing up my shoes tight because in my mind we were going to being chasing this kid.

Every bond I write costs me money whether I receive a dime or not I have to pay the surety their premium. If this kid doesn't have his money, he just costs me money. If I agree to do your bond and take less down then what it cost me to write it, is one thing but to cost me money on false pretense is another. Nobody likes to lose money and I don't like being lied to. I warned this kid on the jail phone that if it wasn't as he said I would return him back to the jail. I made sure we were clear on that. I also told him that it cost me money to post his bail and I cannot afford to be paying for random people to get out of jail.

I told him I have a family to support and gave him plenty of opportunity to change his mind if he was indeed planning on pulling a fast one. We pulled up to his house and I let him out of the back, staying close to him as he walked up to the door. The first lie emerges, he doesn't live with his grandparents. They were elderly but they rented him a room and wanted him to move out. They were shocked to see him walk up and they also looked disappointed that he was out.

He starts walking through the house quickly, hands still cuffed in the front, and runs up the stairs to the second floor. We tried to stay with him, but the homeowners were trying to talk to us and got in the way just enough for him to get to his room and shut and lock the door. I can see on Megan's face, she is understanding the importance of cuffing people in the back no matter their size, appearance or demeanor.

We are dealing with criminals; they don't have a reputation for always being honest and trustworthy. I am in no way saying that every person who gets arrested is dishonest. However, in my years in bail, I've run into more than a few dishonest defendants.

We are all criminals if you sit down and read the hundreds of thousands of laws on the law books. We all break the law in some form or another, most of us are just lucky enough to never get caught. I admit some crimes are petty and aren't worth pursuing and some should be removed from the books all together. In one county I worked in, you could legally beat your wife on the courthouse steps on Sunday afternoon.

We break into the room to see the window open, and he is gone. This kid jumped from a two-story window handcuffed in the front and was nowhere in sight. Talk about determination and stupidity. Well, if there's one thing Megan and I succeeded at doing that night, it was finding something to get into. Now we are chasing a runner.

This kid is about to find out how serious I am about my money and being a woman of my word. Lucky for us he wasn't smart enough to use fake addresses on his application. The elderly couple told us his girlfriend lived across the woods, so we looked up the address he put on our application for his girlfriend in google maps, and sure enough she was on the other side of the woods.

We got in our car and headed over to the girlfriend's house. We watched the house for a few minutes to get an idea of who was living at the address. We see a man in the garage working on a motorcycle and a woman came out with a small dog in tow. They spoke for a few minutes and then they both went back into the house.

We decided then to knock on the door and speak with the parents and let them know what had just happened to their daughter's boyfriend and that we believed he was headed to their house. We asked for permission to be in their backyard to take him back into custody. Dad didn't seem to care for the boy, but mom seemed to feel sorry for him.

The girlfriend came out and talked with us in the back yard with her mother. We found out she was sixteen and possibly pregnant. By this time the sun has set and it's dark in the yard. The backyard backed up to the woods he ran into and that we were expecting him to appear from. She asks us if we will at least let her see him for a minute, which we agreed. We then tell her and her mother to go up to the house and once we had him in custody, they could come speak with him.

We were hidden at the edge of the woods and waited for what seemed like an hour for him to make his way through the dark woods. We started to hear leaves rustling and could hear him making his way right to us. My heart started racing, suddenly, I couldn't hear anything over my heartbeat.

We wait for him to get right up on us, and we jumped out from behind the trees. We have our taser lit up on him ready to fire if he made one wrong move. I went to remove my cuffs and place them in the back, and I realized he didn't have my cuffs on. This guy has some nerve, he first takes me for the cost of writing his bond, he wastes my time hunting him down and he took my cuffs off and threw them in the woods. Absolutely no respect, just selfish actions from another addict.

You would think things like this would deter me from wanting to help the next guy out and in a sense it does. I learn from every experience. Part of me had to know where this kids' real family was and what his back story was. When taking him back to jail he shared some of the traumas he suffered as a child. The story was too horrific to believe, and you truly never know what the truth is.

Megan and I did some research and found out he was indeed telling the truth about his childhood. At a very young age he witnessed his father kill his mother. His father was sentenced to forty years with eighteen years suspended. He walks a free man today.

A few days later he did call and apologize to me for what he had done. He was going to jail for some time and just wanted to see his girlfriend one last time. He would refer me good bonds every chance he got, to make up for what he had cost me, until he was released. He then gave me a five-star review on my business page.

CHAPTER 14

FANTASY

Business was going well, and I was building friendships with the competitors, and they were noticing the benefits of my social media marketing. Everyone who skipped bail to this point, had been picked up. I hope the ones betting against me in the beginning of my career didn't lose too much money. I always wondered if any of them were betting for me? My next case, the craziest failure to appear I have ever bonded out of jail. Whenever I would get a domestic abuse related call, it would take me back to my own case. Domestic abuse cases are hard to prosecute due to the fact there are so many elements involved.

Mainly the emotional connection between the defendant and the victim. As was the case in my own personal experience. I was unable to testify against my boyfriend in our domestic and his charges were dropped. Our relationship had ended over my first year in the bail bond work.

I just didn't have the time to waste to be with someone who couldn't keep his hands to himself, and the drinking wasn't going to stop. I was thankful to that man for one thing. He was always afraid he would be the one to walk in and find my son dead. One day that became his reality. He came in from work and two of my sons' friends had just run out of the house. He went to my sons' room and my son was in bed, his lips turning blue, he wasn't breathing. My son had overdosed, and I was at the jail in Stafford forty-five minutes away posting a bail.

He called 911 and had them on speakerphone while he picked my son up and started shaking him and then proceeded to do CPR until the rescue squad arrived. These two never got along, if you remember my son cut this man's arms up and was charged with assaulting him and now the man, he couldn't stand to be in the same room with was saving his life. If he hadn't come home when he did, I would have lost my son.

He wasn't a good man to me however he saved my son, and I will always be grateful. This domestic case was different in more ways than one. In nine out of ten domestic cases, the victim is the female. In this case the victim was male, he was assaulted by his girlfriend.

After her arrest, he went through his emotions and didn't want to see her go back to jail so he decided to not show up to testify against her, thinking they would just drop the case. The judge continued the case and issued a "show cause" failure to appear on the victim. The best choice to make is to always appear in court. You can always refuse to testify or plead the fifth, but you must be there. Even if your attorney tells you that you don't need to appear because they are continuing the case, go to court!

I have seen attorneys too many times in court, tell judges they don't know where their client is knowing damn well, they told them their appearance wasn't necessary. Being a victim myself of domestic abuse, I understood the challenges he faced. I was shocked that the courts arrested a victim. I had never seen this before and I had never seen it again after this case. Not to say it never happened.

He gave me his friends' information and I set up the bond. His bond was small, set at $1,500 so he had that in his favor. I couldn't help but feel compassion for his situation. I too struggled with whether I should or shouldn't go to court. The thought of going to court gave me anxiety.

When he came out the door, my first impression was he was a happy hippy surfer kid from the west coast. He was about twenty-four years old, and you could tell no matter what, this guy is one of those that makes the best out of his situation. He had such a positive vibe that it radiated the room. If you hadn't seen him walk out of the release door you would have never known, he had just experienced sitting in jail.

I spoke to him for about forty-five minutes in the lobby. I explained to him that no matter what, you must go to court. I explained to him that the state cannot prosecute someone when they cannot produce a witness against them. He could elect his right to plead the fifth or just tell the prosecution he would not testify. They have no choice; they must drop the case. I felt confident after having our conversation that we were on the same page, and I wouldn't have an issue with him appearing in court. A month later the sheriff comes knocking on the door. It's a show cause for my happy hippy surfer kid.

He failed to appear again! I don't like being served with show causes. I don't like the police coming to my door any more than the next person. I have nothing against them personally, but they never bring good news. I support the men and women in blue it's an incredibly hard job to do, and I can't take that away from them. The court date is three weeks away, so I have some time to get him into custody and get the show cause dismissed. I get my paperwork in order and visit the magistrate once more to get yet another Bail Piece signed.

I started calling the fugitive and of course was getting no answer. I sent some text letting him know we can take care of it; I just needed him to contact me so he could turn himself in and I would get him back out. It's Friday night and it's warm outside. Its spring and spring fever has kicked in. Bars were filling up, parties were happening, people were ready to get out of their houses after being cooped up all winter. You could tell when spring fever hit because of the uptick in alcohol related charges at the jail. I get Megan and another female agent together and we decide to send him a text from a number he doesn't know. He had never met Megan or this other agent, so we sent him a text inviting him to a private party.

We attached a photo of them and claimed we had met him at another party two weeks earlier. He responds! I'm thinking, Fish on y'all!

We had a short dialogue through text. It didn't take much to get him to the house, just asked if he was interested in a threesome. I must admit, it seemed too easy. I mean, he must know he is being set up. He asks for the address, and we send him to the other agents' house, which was one block from the jail I needed to return him to.

He responds with "on my way!" This is too good to be true, he is going to come right to me. The girls and I get ready for his arrival. We talk about how to get him to the bedroom as soon as he enters the house. We needed him secured as quickly as possible, we had no idea if he was armed but from what I remembered of him, he was harmless.

The bedroom was right off the main room of the house. They just had to get him through one room and in order to do that Megan would stay in the bedroom as the other agent let him in the door and led him back to the room where the "party" was. I would be in the closet waiting for them to come in. We had set cameras up in case something went bad. I like to record captures in case someone tries to imply I have done something unethical and they're also great training videos.

My job was always to keep my agents safe, the public safe, if the recovery was at a public location, and make sure the defendants were not harmed. We see headlights come up the driveway, so I head to the bedroom to get into position. It's show time y'all! Now I don't recommend anyone, trying this stunt without professional training. Inviting a wanted man in the home not knowing if he was armed was extremely risky.

Megan was sitting on the bed and the other agent answered the door. I can hear her inviting him in and they're headed to the bedroom. Suddenly, I heard another man's voice. I don't know this voice. He brought a friend with him! This is not good; I know nothing about this other guy. A threesome is three people not four, why would you bring another guy?

This made no sense to me, maybe he was afraid to meet us alone. I hear Megan's voice change a bit when she realizes we are dealing with two men now. In my mind we still have them outnumbered. We have no choice but to complete our task. Megan had a code phrase that when she said it, I knew he was in front of the closet door with his back to me. His interest would be directed to the direction of the bed. I'm in the closet hoping she knows when to say it now that there is another man there.

I can't have that guy in my way. The girls were smart enough to maneuver the friend out of the way and had him sitting in a chair in the opposite corner of the room. Megan says the code phrase and I swing the closet door open. He jumps and turns toward the closet to see me standing there with taser in hand. His friend is backed up against the wall across the room in a chair. He put his hands up and smiled and said you got me. He said I knew this was too good to be true. His friend agrees with his statement, also displaying a very laid-back demeanor.

As I am securing him, I'm talking to the friend letting him know the process and what was going on. I needed everyone to stay calm and go with the flow. I don't want to shoot someone with a taser. I just want off the bond and clear up my show cause. The mood was light, and nobody was getting hostile. The fugitive asked if we could get a photo together, so the girls and I took our picture with him while he was cuffed.

We took him to the jail and the magistrate revoked his bond. He had to sit in jail until he got another bond through a judge. A week later he called me from jail, and he got his bond back. He asked me to bond him again, and I did, however I made him put his car up for collateral.

He failed to appear again, so I took his car that he used as collateral to get out and I picked him up again at a courthouse parking lot, where I expected him to be, testifying for his girlfriend who had more charges. That was the last time I did business with him. He caught more charges and bonded out through another company and again he didn't go to court. He just didn't like going to court, which is the worst kind of client to have in bail.

CHAPTER 15

PIZZA BOY

I am moving right along navigating this new career. I was building my business page that was instrumental in keeping my business alive. One of the things I enjoyed the most was helping agents with hard-to-find fugitives. I was making my daily calls to the agents, checking on everyone and getting our day started. While on the phone with one of the agents, I call daily, he tells me about this fugitive, I call pizza boy, who slipped out of a small basement window on them the night before. The fugitive ran on a $30,000 bond. That will put you out of business quickly.

This sounded like something I wanted to get into. He tells me they're going out that evening to look for him again, so I offer my help and he accepts. We all met up at his office and we decided we would retrace steps from the night before. The fugitive was working for a pizza delivery chain, so we started there.

Another agent and I went in and ordered a pizza and sat in the lobby watching every worker there until our pizza was ready, and we had to leave so we didn't blow our cover, he was not there. We went to the house where he was renting a room and where he had slipped out of the tiny basement window. We interviewed them to see if they had any information as to where he might be, and they had no information to share.

The family living there claimed they had not seen him since he left the day before. We had no reason not to believe them. They didn't seem like the fugitive harboring type of people. They were a small family; they had a couple of kids and had rented a room to the wrong person. We moved on to some relatives listed on the application. The one name that kept being mentioned at every house we went to, was his friend Daniel. It caught my attention because my oldest son is named Daniel.

We headed back to the vehicles, and I asked one of the agents if he was on the fugitive's Facebook page and he replied yes, but he keeps posting that he is in different places all over the state. I tell them we need to get back to the office, and they need to put me on his page. We arrived at the office, and I got on his Facebook page. The agent was only looking at his post hoping this guy would tell him where he was. That does happen however this guy was using his page to take someone on a wild chase that would never lead to fruition.

I went straight to his friends list and there he was, Daniel. I was thankful that he had only one friend named Daniel. I told the other agent to pull a background check on Daniel on his page. The kid was living with his parents who have been in their home for over thirty years. They still had a land line, and we had found their number through the background check, so we made a call.

The parents answer the phone, and we explain to them who we are. We asked them if their son had a friend staying with him and they replied yes. We tell the parents the person with their son is a wanted fugitive and that we are on our way to pick him up. We asked them to not let the son or friend know we were coming, and they said they would be waiting for us.

The address is about thirty minutes from the office, and I got a bond call for my company, so I had to back out at this time and head to the jail. I helped them locate him, which was the best thing I could offer at that time, and forty-five minutes later they called to let me know he was in custody!

Another one bites the dust! I was able to prove myself worthy to some agents who had ten years or more on me. Now they owed me one, and I would cash in one day.

CHAPTER 16

THE METH LAB

It's business as usual, another day another dollar. I received a call from a name that's all too familiar. This guy was one of my subcontractors back when I owned a floorcovering company. I know that when he called my company that he had no idea he was calling me. I ask him all the usual questions to prequalify the bond, I ask him about his employment, and he tells me he installs flooring. That's when I knew it was him. I tell him who I am, and he remembers working for me years ago.

I could tell by the charges he was dealing with substance abuse issues however at this time he had been in jail for over six months and sounded like he was thinking more clearly. I called his family, and we scheduled a time to post his bond. When I owned my floor-covering business, I was good to my subcontractors. I just knew he wasn't going to give me a hard time. He was going to stay out of trouble, stay off the drugs and go to court until the case was finalized.

A few months went by, and he had been going to all his court appearances. Defendants will appear for all their court dates until they get to the one where they know a decision is being made, and they're going back in and that is the case with my client.

He had continued his case a few times and was scheduled to take a plea. He knew his next court appearance he was going back in, so he failed to appear. As expected, the sheriff came to see me again and served me with a show cause. I cannot even describe to you how angry I was when I saw his name on the paperwork. I tried to call him, and his phone was shut off. I then found out that the person who signed him out of jail has passed away and therefore I have no one to secure this bond. I can't reach him, and I can't reach anyone on his application.

I get on my page and post him up as a fugitive. Sometimes this approach would work in getting them to call you and handle it and other times it was just a formality that led to the chase. People didn't normally like being posted to the page and I didn't like losing money, so I felt like it evened the playing field.

Every person I bonded out of jail knew if they failed to appear on my bond they would be posted to my page. My page had a huge following and was instrumental in the capture of about ninety percent of the fugitives posted. I was so angry about the disrespect he had shown towards me, so he was being posted every day sometimes several times a day. The leads started rolling in and I felt like I had enough information to hit the road and find him.

Megan and I loaded up and headed south to where all the leads were coming from. It was a hot Saturday afternoon in late spring. The weather was clear, and it was a good day to hunt. We followed every lead and hit every address given to me from leads from my business page. One lead, we felt was a good starting point, because it came from one of my sons' friends who was using meth. He claimed to have been at the house with the "toothless cougar" as they called her, and my fugitive was living there and cooking shake and bake meth.

Megan and I arrived at this run down double wide that was off an old country dirt road. The driveway was about a half mile long and lined with thick trees on either side, it felt like we were headed deep in the woods. The yard was littered with trash, broken down vehicles scattered throughout, burn pits, some yard ornaments and a few pit bulls tied up in various places around the house. I took the front and Megan took the back. We had each other on our phones and ear buds in so we could communicate with one another.

I knock on the door and this old frail woman answers the door. She couldn't have weighed more than ninety pounds. She was missing all her teeth and her clothes were very revealing. I could see two young men in the background, they couldn't have been much older than eighteen. I tell the woman we need to search the house because we were given information that our fugitive was there. Surprisingly, she granted us permission, I walked straight through to the back door to let Megan in the house. The woman followed us around the house, throwing out information as we walked through each room. She informed us that my fugitive was there, and he indeed was making meth, however his dog had gotten into it and died, and my fugitive left and hadn't come back to the house. She claimed it had been at least three days since she had last seen him.

A few moments later after we had cleared the house, Megan notices her texting someone. We asked her not to use her phone while we were there for safety reasons. She shows Megan the phone and "says, it's just one of my boy toys'. Megan realizes she is talking to the informant that sent us there. The woman then stakes claim to her toothless cougar's name and said, "didn't you know, they call me the Toothless Cougar?" She then gave us the biggest grin, showing all her gums with pride.

Oh, we knew, we just had to see it to believe it. She completely changed the meaning of cougar for me. With no fugitives in sight, we pack up and move forward with our plan to hit the next address on our list. The second house we hit had another client of mine living there. My client tells me that my fugitive has a pattern of where he walks to everyday and if I watch the main road, I will eventually see him walking up and down it.

He was homeless and supposedly staying in the small patch of woods behind this townhouse. We received permission to search the house, and cleared every inch, but again he was not there. Hey, you got to keep them honest and make sure you're not being fed lies to go away. I don't like my time wasted just like the next person.

I let my client, that was living at this address, know that if he was feeding us lies, I would be back to pick him up and revoke his bond. Megan and I decide to go into the woods and see if we can find any evidence to validate these claims. There was a walking path through the woods from the townhouses that led to a playground. You could hear children in the distance enjoying the playground on this hot day. We had been all over the county looking for him with no luck. As we were looking through the small patch of trees, we came across what looked like a pile of trash. After further examining it, we realized it was a shake and bake meth lab.

I called the county and explained who we were and what we were doing and made dispatch aware of the lab we had just found and asked if they would send an officer out. They declined to do so. Megan and I decided we are going to move this stuff. It was right off the path that children take to the playground, not to mention people's pets could also get into it and get hurt. It was too dangerous to leave there. We were also aware of the danger of transporting a meth. lab. I took photos before we touched anything and posted to my business page that I found his shake and bake lab and was getting close. Megan and I bagged it all up and put it in my trunk. My entire car was taking on this awful meth smell.

We both knew the dangers of transporting it and getting caught but we were also aware that a dog had just died getting into this stuff and didn't want to see another animal or person hurt because of his reckless actions. I would have felt responsible if that had happened so the benefit of moving it outweighed the risk.

We needed to find the safest place to dispose of this stuff where no one could get hurt. We drive around until we locate a dumpster at an apartment complex with a trash compactor on it. We dumped the bag in the dumpster and turned the compactor on.

Bad Girlz Bail Bonds llc.

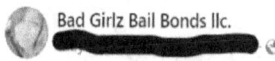

Well I'm getting close ▆▆▆ you left in such a hurry that you forgot your meth lab! Kids could have gotten a hold of this stuff or someone's pet..what would you care though, you killed your own dog with this stuff! Too bad the police can't prove its yours or you would be catching some more felonies right now!

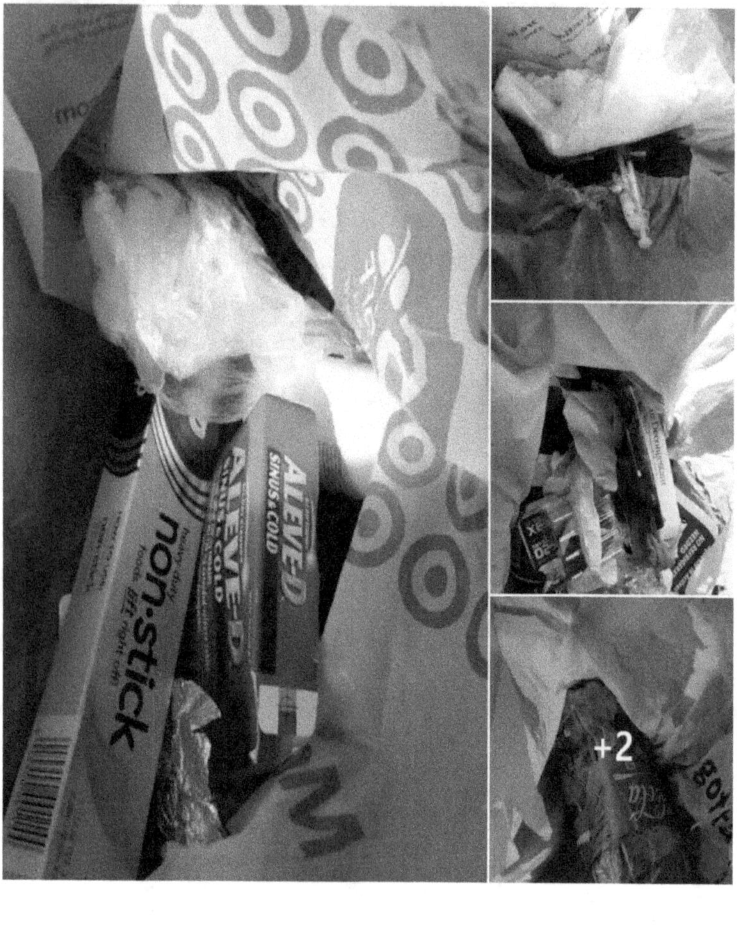

We were getting tired; we had been going all day. We stopped at WAWA to get some water and some fresh watermelon while we discussed our next move. Both of us were feeling exhausted and defeated and ready for our long ride back home. I hated the ride home empty handed, its like a walk of shame.

We sat in the WAWA parking lot for about twenty minutes trying to make the call and had finally decided to pack up and go home. On the way back home, we had to drive down the road my other client claimed I would see him walking on. I tell Megan to pull into the Lowes parking lot. I just wanted to drive through the shopping center and see if by chance we would see him.

She pulls up to the lumber side of Lowes, which was on the right end of the shopping center and there he is! At that exact moment, I see him walking into the lumber side entrance of Lowes. I didn't hesitate, I grabbed my taser from the floor of the car and I jumped from the vehicle before Megan could come to a complete stop. I couldn't let him get too far in Lowes or lose sight of him.

A Lowes employee sees me coming and apparently follows my page. He yells out "get him bad girl". I ran as fast and as quietly as I could to catch up to my fugitive. By this time, he was walking the main aisle in the front of the store in front of the registers. I came up behind him slowly and with taser drawn and pressing in his back, I told him to get on the ground.

He complied with my every command and was cuffed in no time. Everything happened so fast, and nobody was injured. By this time Megan had parked the car and joined me in walking him out. We were keeping a fast pace and trying not to make a scene, so people didn't realize what had just happened.

As we walked him out the employee at the lumber door who recognized me told me he was about to call me and tell me he was in the store to get the reward, then he started singing "Bad Girlz Bad Girlz, what Cha going to do, when they come for you. "I cannot tell you how many times that phrase would get sung to me over the years.

We get him loaded up and head back to Manassas Jail. We were both exhausted and just wanted to drop him off and go home but that wasn't going to happen just yet. Megan had offered to feed him before we took him in.

I admit, he looked like he hadn't eaten in a while, and we all know the food in jail isn't that appetizing. We pulled through a McDonald's drive-thru and even though he had screwed me over financially, we fed him. We then allowed him to have a cigarette outside the jail before walking him in intake. That man stayed in and out of jail. He was eventually bonded with another company, which he failed to appear in court.

Photo credit: Megan Wilson

Picture taken in the Lowes parking lot after he was taken into custody.

CHAPTER 17

RUNAWAY

I was nearing the end of my second full year as a bail bond agent. My page was growing, and my business was growing as well. I had expanded and added an agent this year and we were getting noticed across the country. To this date, I haven't been paid for any recoveries, rather they cost me. It was the second week of December and I saw a post on Facebook regarding a local runaway. This type of case was something I had never dealt with. The girl was sixteen years old and was talking with an older man.

The mom suspected drug abuse and was also concerned her daughter was going to be trafficked and moved to the state of Georgia. The man she was allegedly with had a criminal record, that included various felony charges. We had enough information to know we were dealing with a career criminal. This seemed like a dangerous situation for her daughter to be in, so I offered to help the mother.

I ask her for every detail she can give me regarding her daughter and the man in question. I also needed any photos she may have of them. I let her know that I would be posting all information and photos I receive to my page and that I would offer a reward out of my pocket for any information leading to the whereabouts of her daughter.

Other than paying the reward, the only services I could provide was to locate her daughter and notify her and the local authorities of all the information I had gathered about the case. I stipulated that the reward would only be paid if she was returned home before Christmas. Christmas was always a difficult time of the year for me, and this year was no different. I was struggling to buy my kids Christmas presents and here I am offering up money I couldn't afford to give away.

As with any commissioned careers, you have your great months, good months and bad months. The problem is you never knew what kind of month you were going to have until that month was over. I had my own issues going on at home with my children and I had a $20,000 skip that I had to either pay the bond or find him by 2nd of January.

It's hard to shop for Christmas when you may get hit with a $20,000 forfeiture the week after. The pressure was on, I needed to find this girl, find this fugitive, and post enough bail to be able to provide a Christmas for my kids. It would be my Christmas miracle if I could pull it all off. I instantly get to work on both cases, putting my wanted posters and rewards online. Legally, I cannot go to the man's house that the runaway was supposedly at and kick his door in and remove her daughter. Even if I saw her go into his house. She was a runaway not a fugitive and the man she was allegedly with was not a fugitive as well. I did make a promise to bring this woman's daughter home by Christmas and being a woman of my word, I had to put all my effort forth to do just that. When I started posting about her daughter, I was getting zero responses. As we started getting closer to Christmas, and I had nothing, no information at all on her or my fugitive, I started to lose faith. I decided to raise the reward money. When I did within minutes a lead came in on my runaway.

It was the lead I needed to know exactly where she was at that moment. The call came from someone inside the home she was hiding in. I called her mother, and I called the county police and forwarded the information to them as I was headed to the location. I needed to meet the informant to pay them for the information, however they were not getting paid until the mother confirmed with me that she had her daughter returned to her. I parked about a block away and I could see the lights on the police cars, but my view was pretty much blocked other than that. The mother was on the scene, and she kept me updated through messenger. I waited for what seemed like an eternity, in fact it had only been a few minutes before I receive the call I've been waiting for. Her daughter had been located and was turned over to the mother.

I then contacted the informant and had them meet me down the street to pay them the reward money. It was hard on me handing over that cash because of my own financial problems, however I knew what I was doing was right and you can't go wrong, doing right. As soon as I finished up my business with them my cell phone rang, it was a large bond with all the premium and a great signer. Before I could leave the area, I had made the reward money back that I had just given away plus some.

The mother and I kept in contact for years. She supported my business by sharing my posts and telling people about what I had done for her. After this case I had considered becoming a private investigator (PI) and hunting runaways but for now, I'm sticking to bail and fugitive recovery. Now the only thing left to do to finish off a great year, was find my elusive $20,000 fugitive coming due for payment.

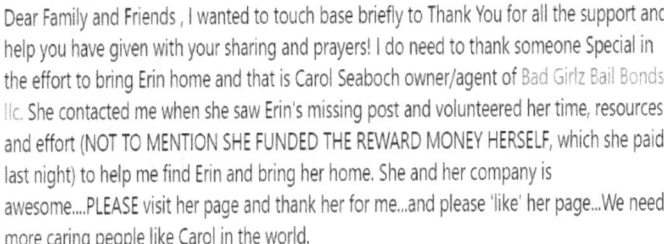

CHAPTER 18

MY CHRISTMAS GIFT

The year is quickly coming to an end, and I have one fugitive, a $20,000 skip that I had to pick up before the 2nd of January. I had him posted for weeks with no response, so I decided to double the reward to $500 a few days before Christmas. Everyone needs Christmas cash; it was worth a shot. I'd rather pay someone $500 than pay $20,000 to the court. I had been calling his mom who claimed she had no idea where he was. I tried to explain to her that she owed me $20,000 if we didn't find him. She acts as if she doesn't understand what I'm saying, so I reference the paperwork.

She knew English very well when she was bonding him out of jail and now, she wants to play this language barrier game. I knew I was wasting my time and needed to move on because I had no time to waste. I had just found a runaway the night before and could focus all my attention on my case. I posted my fugitive again and got a hit. He was in my town, hanging out in this woman's apartment. She had kids and they also needed Christmas presents.

I get the address and Megan and I head over to the apartment complex to do surveillance. The informant requested that I take him when he leaves her place. She was fearful he would find out she was the one that turned him in. We sat in our car for hours and every twenty minutes or so we would get a glimpse of our fugitive on her patio smoking. We realized he had a broken foot, which means it was very doubtful there was going to be a chase. He was, however, involved with a gang which was concerning and some of the members were in the apartment as well.

This wasn't something Megan and I felt comfortable doing without back up, so I called in one of my favors. I had been helping other agents, it's time I got help. We sat in the car, me having to pee for about an hour now, watching people come and go from that apartment.

When help finally arrives, I tell the guys I'm going to a bathroom across the street at pizza hut and we would be right back. We had been sitting there for five and a half hours and when you're sitting in a car with nothing to do you tend to snack and drink soda. We return and the guys who have only been there for maybe fifteen minutes are ready to hit the apartment. I told them that I gave my word to her that we would not get him there. We sit there for about an hour, the guys complaining the entire time, it's midnight and we all want to go home. I start messaging the informant and telling her, I'm sorry, I can no longer wait; we must come in and get him.

Megan and I had been there for about seven hours, the guys had been there maybe two and were ready to leave. She lets me know the door is unlocked and finally the moment I had been waiting for, for over six months, has arrived. I'm going to get this guy; I'm not going to lose $20,000 and my company will continue to do business as usual. We approach the door; the two male agents were in front on this one. We walk right in with authority, announce who we are, the male agents had their guns drawn, I had the handcuffs ready. He was sitting at the dining room table when we grabbed him up and took him out of there.

The safest thing we can do is grab and go. We had his friends and fellow gang members following us down the three flights of stairs. It was my job to keep the friends back while Megan had run before us to pull the car up so we could get in and go. We got him in our car, and this is when the other agents left us to transport him by ourselves. We had to take him to a jail that was over two hours away and the guys were not willing to transport the fugitive with us.

He had a broken foot and realized the gig was up, so he didn't give us any issues. The only issue we had to overcome during this recovery was with intake at the jail. They were trying to refuse to take him into custody because of his broken foot. Now I've taken people to jail with some new injuries and understood the process of getting them medical treatment prior to bringing them in but he had a cast on. This injury was old, he didn't need medical attention. It's 3:00 a.m. and I have no patience for this nonsense. I asked the corrections officer if he was going to go in front of the judge and tell him that he turned a fugitive away because he had a foot in a cast? I let him know I was going to mention his name, which was placed on his shirt, when I had to appear on the 2nd of January.

We had all the proper paperwork, there was no need for all this. We sat at the sally port door while he went to speak to his supervisor. About twenty minutes later, they appeared with a wheelchair and took custody of him.

I appeared in court on the 2nd of January and handed the judge my signed bail piece. I promised the judge at my last court appearance that if he would continue the matter and allow me an extra thirty days, I would recover him, and I did. It felt great walking out of that courtroom. Everyone in the courtroom had some sense of respect for my work. I cannot describe that feeling other than accomplished and respected.

CHAPTER 19

THE SPLIT AND RECONCILIATION

Megan and I worked great together for a few months. We were picking up fugitives left and right. We were like peanut butter and jelly, can't have one without the other. I had her trained on posting bail, qualifying a bond and recovery. One day we had a blowout fight. I cannot for the life of me remember what it was about, and I called her when writing this book to ask her, her perspective. Her response was "We were having our yearly fight." We had yearly arguments, as we called them.

It's like we would spend too much time together and then blow up on each other. We can never remember what we were fighting over after a little time passed. That tells you how important they were. Megan and I were going our separate ways in business and were no longer on speaking terms. Never in a million years would I have expected what she did next.

I understand we all need to make a living. Megan was no exception to this rule, and I knew that by no longer working for me she would become my competition. I'm sitting in the jail, and she walks in to post a bond. I looked over and saw her paperwork and I couldn't help but notice the company logo. It was all too familiar.

Megan accepted a position with the company I began my career with. Not only was she working for the competition, but she also chose the one company I despised the most. We didn't speak for several months; I just couldn't talk to her and her to me. When we were both at the jail the tension was so intense, you could cut it with a knife. Then one day I noticed a new company on Facebook, and I saw the same company listed at the jails I worked at. I started asking agents if they knew who was behind this new company. Nobody knew who they were.

We would have companies that would have five or six lines with different names all going to the same agent. I had to do some investigating, so I went to the company's page and started talking crap, accusing them of not being licensed and asking them to identify themselves and prove they are indeed licensed. It's the best way to get information sometimes and it worked.

I finally got the answer I was looking for; the owner of the new agency was Megan. She had left the slime ball and started her own agency. I cannot fault her for that at all. She was trying to make a living. We started talking again and I ended up putting her on my surety so she could make more than what her other surety was offering. Making a higher percentage meant she didn't have to write every bond that came in on her phoneline and she could be more selective, and it also gave her more time with her dying husband.

We made a deal to post each other's bail for a flat fee as needed or when possible and we started to do recovery's together again because even though she wasn't an agent for Bad Girlz anymore she was writing on my surety under me, making me liable for what she was writing. Look out y'all were back and better than before!

CHAPTER 20

HANDICAPPED AND ELDERLY

    I was sitting at Stafford jail with another agent, who became a close friend to me. She was a seasoned agent that had fifteen more years in the business than I did, and I respected her advice. We were talking about different stuff we have going on, and she asks me if I'm willing to help her grab this elderly crippled woman. I don't hesitate to help; how hard could this be? We both finish posting our bonds and finish up with our clients, it's still early in the afternoon. I remember the sun was shining and it was warm outside, perfect weather for a recovery.

She takes me to this single wide trailer out in the country sitting in a small trailer park. We pulled right up to the trailer, there was no hiding the fact that we were there, she is crippled and elderly. We thought it was highly unlikely the woman would see us and evade. We could get around faster and better than her, so we had the advantage.

We went to the door and her daughter answered. We tell her we are taking her mother to jail for failure to appear. Her mother was sitting on the couch in the living room in plain sight. The mother asks us as sweet as can be if she can just get her shoes on and get her things together like her medications. The trailer had a smell of male cat spray so strong it was hard to stand in the doorway. So, the other agent and I decided to let her put her shoes on and we closed the glass door and stepped down from the porch to the driveway waiting for her to appear.

While we were out in the driveway, and since it was such a beautiful day, we decided to take some selfies in front of the trailer. Suddenly, this man appeared, we could tell he was watching us, giving us looks like we were crazy, and us back at him, like mind your own business. We had even made some smart comments amongst each other about it.

We then realized it's been about ten to fifteen minutes and she hadn't come out, so we went back to the door. Her daughter answers and says she isn't here. Wait, what? Impossible she was a handicapped woman and couldn't walk. The other agent nor I wanted to go in the trailer. It was a hoarding situation; stuff was everywhere, and the floor wasn't safe to walk across. We tell her daughter that we are going to call the county out here since she is wanted and let them search the trailer.

We call Spotsylvania County, and they show up four cars deep. I always loved doing recoveries in Spotsylvania because they were always willing to assist, ran deep and would bring dogs. We were not allowed to use dogs for recoveries. Spotsylvania cops clear inside the trailer and under it, the woman was gone. The four officers, who know us well looked at us both and said "really, y'all let a crippled elderly woman get away?" We took a little heat from them, and we were their comic relief for the day. Hell, we couldn't stop laughing at ourselves. What a rookie mistake we had made. We did our agent walk of shame and drove back to my car replaying the events and cracking up at the mistake we made not covering the back door and swearing we would never tell anyone this happened. We also were on a mission to catch her.

The next day, the agent called and said she had a lead that she was in a hotel. We decided to meet up down the street and set up in the parking lot of the hotel. The information she had received included a room number, so we knew where to be watching. We see the daughter exit the room to get ice and know it's good information. We decided to hit it as soon as the daughter returned to the room.

The daughter gets back in the room and the agent, and I walk up and knock on the door. The daughter answers and we let her know we are coming into that room for her mother. The room isn't big, and it doesn't take long. The other agent looked in the bathroom and then turned around to walk away and then turned back around again to go back to the bathroom. She pulled the shower curtain back, and I heard the agent scream! As soon as I heard the agent scream, I knew we were redeemed. The elderly handicapped woman was hiding in the shower. The agent tells her to get out of the shower and come on.

We get her in handcuffs, and she tells us she can't walk and that we need to carry her or help her by letting her lean on us. The agent and I looked at each other and then looked at her and said, "you walked, crawled, ran just fine yesterday, you're walking your ass to the truck."

Looking back, we can both laugh about it, and we tell the story to anyone who wants to hear it. Sometimes you must just laugh at your mistakes and then learn from them. That's the important part.

CHAPTER 21

GETTING NOTICED

    I never imagined my business and my social media reach would grow to the extent it had in such a short period of time. My marketing was paying off and I noticed other agents trying to build their own business pages as well. I admit, at first it kind of angered me, then I realized imitation is the best form of flattery. I would show them support and follow their pages and share their fugitive post when asked. I admit, when I first got in the business and during the first year, I would wear a vest, handcuffs, taser and all the gear.

I didn't have a firearm until mid-2012, which I didn't carry long, I felt more comfortable carrying a non-lethal weapon so I could pull the trigger if needed and not have to worry about possibly killing someone.

Putting the gear on became a part of my ritual of getting ready for a hunt. I had a playlist I would play and share to my page while I was getting ready, hunting, and music I would share when they were caught. I wouldn't even have to tell people on my page what I was doing, they would know by the song I would post on social media, and they would get ready for what was about to be posted. Every fugitive caught would get posted to the page as well.

I would play Disturbed, "Down with The Sickness" when I was getting ready, it always got me pumped up. When I was on the hunt, I would share Styx "Renegade Man" and when they were caught, I would share Queen, "Another One Bites the Dust." We realized people didn't like talking to us much when we wore all that gear. We looked too much like cops and people aren't as willing to sit on their porch talking to the police. Especially in the neighborhoods we were frequenting. Megan and I decided to lose the vest and gear.

We would carry a taser in the small part of our back under the waste line of our jeans and cover it with our shirt. We kept handcuffs in our back pocket and the key and badge in the front pocket. We dressed in jeans, t shirts and tennis shoes or boots and tried to appear as nothing more than two women, not two agents.

This worked much better for us in getting information and even though the other agents would lecture us about this all the time, we still felt more comfortable and continued to hunt without the gear. I do not recommend anyone doing this. I knew it wasn't the safest practice, but I also have faith in God, and I knew I wasn't leaving this earth not one second before I am supposed too.

I understood their concerns and the safety aspect, but I also felt, wearing that gear sometimes put a target on our backs, especially if we were confused for being a cop. Dressing as we normally did give us an advantage, most of the time we had our fugitives in custody before they knew what was going on. We started to get noticed all over the country by other bail bond agents and recovery agents. I would be contacted by agents out of state who had cases that ran to my state. I saw an opportunity to expand the business and ran with it.

Megan and I enjoyed hunting, and we were risking our lives doing so, it's about time we started making money for our services. We weren't two big burly guys carrying firearms. We were just two women trying to survive the fast lane in a predominantly male industry. I was happy to hunt so I or another agent wouldn't lose money however some of the hunts could get expensive. Usually if I was hunting with another team, they would cover the expenses however if it was my case, I was covering theirs. We had received requests for several cases before we decided to start taking them.

Our next journey sent us around the country, picking up some of the most dangerous criminals. We traveled from the east to west coast, north to south. We had many exciting, sad and exhausting experiences and seen places we would never have gotten to see otherwise. I have more stories to share, this is the beginning of a series of books, from hunting my own son, the fugitive that got run over by the tractor, the most dangerous fugitive we ever apprehended, and hunting down the love of my life, Moonshiner Tickle.

Watch for Cat the Bounty Huntress Volume two for more real-life bounty hunting stories from the best female bail bond and recovery agent on the East Coast

SOURCES

Carol Tickle, AKA Cat the Bounty Huntress

Megan Wilson Agent

Kim Mack Agent

Bill Weisband

CONTACT INFORMATION-EMAIL
CTicklebooks@gmail.com

PO BOX 96

Callands, VA 24530

www.ingramcontent.com/pod-product-compliance
Lightning Source LLC
Chambersburg PA
CBHW071414210526
45465CB00001B/380